OTHER TITLES FROM AIRLIE PRESS

THE EDDY FENCE   *Donna Henderson*

LAST APPLES OF LATE EMPIRES   *Jessica Lamb*

GARDEN OF BEASTS   *Anita Sullivan*

OUT OF REFUSAL   *Carter McKenzie*

ENTERING   *Cecelia Hagen*

THE NEXT THING ALWAYS BELONGS   *Chris Anderson*

CONGRESS OF STRANGE PEOPLE   *Stephanie Lenox*

IRON STRING   *Annie Lighthart*

STILL LIFE WITH JUDAS & LIGHTNING   *Dawn Diez Willis*

SKEIN OF LIGHT   *Karen McPherson*

PICTURE X   *Tim Shaner*

SETTING THE FIRES   *Darlene Pagán*

PARTLY FALLEN   *Deborah Akers*

WISH MEAL   *Tim Whitsel*

THE CATALOG OF BROKEN THINGS

THE CATALOG OF BROKEN THINGS

A. Molotkov

Airlie Press
PORTLAND OREGON
2016

Airlie Press is supported by book sales, by contributions to the press from its supporters, and by the work donated by all the poet-editors of the press.

Major funding has been provided by, or on behalf of:
Christine Stephenson
Julia Ryan Wills
Anonymous (in honor of Ann and Erik Muller)

P.O. BOX 82653
PORTLAND OR 97282
WWW.AIRLIEPRESS.ORG

EMAIL: EDITORS@AIRLIEPRESS.ORG

Cover Art and Book Design: Beth Ford
Glib Communications & Design, Portland, OR

First Edition
ISBN: 978 0-9895799-3-3
Library of Congress Control Number: 2016937016

Printed in the United States of America

for Laurie

CONTENTS

THE CATALOG OF BROKEN THINGS
1

THE PROTAGONIST'S TRUE STORY
19

THE MELTING HOURGLASS
27

YOUR LIFE AS IT IS
51

THE CATALOG OF BROKEN THINGS

1

I let my dead mother in.
She's lonely out there on her own.
Her ears are seashells
empty of sea.
She carries me among her bones
where her womb was.

The moon, a breath
away, a dead fact.

I leak into the moment, linger.
Death holds
my hand, listens. I want to stop, to go
back, to think
it through before
being.

Shadows watch
out for me.

My mother brings a pillow full of
her own hair, soft like dawn.
She grew it all her life, and after.
She sleeps lighter with her head
on her own past.
The past, her only coin.

Her lips don't move. She says,
Where is your passport?

I don't have it.
I don't need it yet.

Her eyes are flowers, but softer.

2

My wife, an answer
that eludes questions, makes
words shine in their own right and wrong,
turns
thoughts to facts
to fictions, makes me
regret our passing future,
our separate past.

She is a crooked mirror,
in which I'm more
and less.

She undefines me,
sends me looking for myself
in new places.

I invite exile, love
invasion, mourn
her in advance.

3

My father holds a fishing net of small suns,
each shining hesitantly, uncertain
which planets might revolve around it.
He carries his boat.

His eyes are oceans of salt
with rocky islands in the middle
where light goes to sleep.

His hands are heavy from the work.

His lips a crack in darkness.
The moon fails, falls. The wind listens.

4

My uncle's face is askew.
He hasn't been born yet.
His feet are embedded in beautiful marble blocks.

He's ready
to tell me things about my parents
I'd rather never know.

My parents have their own
beautiful marble
blocks. My uncle retreats, uncertain
of my attention.

I'm someone else's memory,
someone else's marble block.

5

My sister wears her old skin,
her face a boat.

If I shake her hand, will
she crumble? She has her passport.
If I embrace her, will she turn
into a shadow in my arms?

6

I see myself in the street, by the sea, in a cell, in a shell, in a joke, in an accident.

I see my life as a short story. As I prepare to vacate my body, my thoughts run after me. My brevity lasts, demands lifelong scrutiny.

7

My son gives away
heaps of roses on a dusty street corner.
His hands bleed from rose thorns,
but he smiles, ruffles his hair,

a garden in his head.

I don't know how
it ends.

8

My grandmother is not
herself.
She has a room of dark fabric.

My brother and I fear to disturb her.
We listen for her
footsteps
when we can't fall
asleep.

She reminds us of all the sad futures we have
escaped. The moon is written on her
face.

9

My father died before
I was conceived.

He sets sail, his winds all his own,
his water, his future, connected in
a certainty, his boat a yes.
He holds the map of broken things.

He seeks the most
irreparable.

I listen to his eyes, relearn
his story, welcome
absence into my life.

I touch my dust, dust my mirrors.

10

My grandfather has wings,
but he doesn't
know it.
He uses them just once, to fly away
before I can
meet him. He is waiting, in his hands
a small sun.
He doesn't seem to notice it.

His smile is glued to his face,
his passport in his pocket,
his feet embedded in a beautiful
marble block.

11

My aunt, a shadow without a landing.
In her chest, small
streams fight for the chance to be
called *river.*
I list her in my catalog under tumors.
She deserves more attention.
We all do, we keep
telling the moon,
but it's dead. It doesn't listen.

I listen.

12

My husband is an ocean
I don't have
a boat for. His thoughts come long
distances to reach me.

He looms in the doorframe
with his gender and his sex and his
confidence.
I could be swept away by his single move,
yet he moves me.

He hurts me without knowing.
He learns me touch
by touch as I
learn him, mourn
him in advance.

13

My daughter's hands are made
of mirrors
reflecting only my own
face.
Is this how she thinks
of me, or I of her?

She is a shadow without offspring.

Her face is missing,
as if I'd never thought
her through.

14

My mother nods in her chair all day.
Her cup is full of air. Her eyes,
so vacant one can
fill them with one's
own hopes.

Silence is her
only coin.

She holds the map of broken things
for my catalog.
She keeps a small, private smile.
Her eyes, kaleidoscopes of darkness.

She knows suns
and moons fail in the end. Boats
sink, rot. Marble
crumbles. And now, I
know it, too. I'm used to this
exit of others, this betrayal
of permanence.

My lips don't move.

I tell her,
That thing you said was true.
I've applied for my passport.

◇ **2** ◇

THE PROTAGONIST'S TRUE STORY

In the final experiment, I am the hope,
and you, the hoped for. The setting
changes according to season and century.
The raindrops are optional.

The protagonist unlocks the door. The house is the same as years ago. Does our story start at birth or maturity? A great idea was just there on the tips of our minds when we bent down for a quarter and a bright future on a sunny street so long ago.

In the final experiment, I am you and you
are I. We meet in the middle of an empty
field. You take out your weapon of choice.
Perhaps it's my choice.

Veins have no traffic lights, no stop signs. Blood laughs at high speeds. Life boils our white cells, runs from the scene of the accident. We are the eggs of our future selves. The protagonist is not in this scene.

Our past is a language only
we can speak, on a good day,
and not fluently.

In the final experiment, the protagonist
is the protagonist. The protagonist enters
hesitantly, aware that the narrative deals
with matters of life and death.

The futures we have not chosen linger like lost fables on burned parchment. Time's gloved hand doesn't touch them. The past and the story don't look each other in the face. The body turns away from its own mistakes, its cancer cells. The protagonist wrapped in a blanket of memories is how we think of our lives.

In the final experiment, I'm the rabbit, and
you, the wheat field. I press my haunches
into your fertile soil, each leap eternal.
You are tender under me. You make many
sounds. The air smells of grass. Then you
are the eagle, your swoop smooth and
elegant, like a long parenthesis. I'm still
the rabbit.

We study ourselves
under bright lights.

Our lives are in a rush to get through their plots, so they can rest. The train
arrives. The house has changed since the beginning of this account. The
dog waits on the chain. The protagonist reclines, slumped in a chair, sleeps
through the bombardment.

In the final experiment, you are death,
and I am life. Your long-term chances are
excellent. You show me to the waiting room.

In the cellar, our tools wait. We know brick, glass, wood, eye, arm, back.
Do we really affect the outcome? Cancer cells don't sleep. We extend our
arms into space, mold it to our will. But not our own stories. We love it
all. A flood starts, a flood ends. We fall asleep with each other's names on
our lips.

In the final experiment, you tell me not to
come, but I do. When I arrive, you are not
there. I step out to look for you. When you
arrive, I'm not here. You step out to look
for me. We never see each other again.

We swim as far as there
is ocean to believe in.

The day starts without us, its lurid blanket of light like a gloved hand on our throats when we wake. Our eyes burst open like eggs, committing us to this reason without reason. Like a needle, the protagonist penetrates the day: agendas of office, shop, field, forest. The setting doesn't matter. It's always the right season. A great idea lingers in the air.

> In the final experiment, you are the typist,
> and I'm the letter *I*. Each time you press
> my key, your finger applies more pressure.
> Then you type out a vehement line of *I*'s to
> make a point.

Moon sleeps, sun rests. Before too long, we don't bother to check which is in charge. The protagonist wrapped in a blanket of memories is our gift to ourselves. Our own story must be past its middle. How lucky, to have survived. Have we done well for ourselves, for others? The day ends without us. Night arrives before we look up to notice. Our future is no less bright in the dark.

> *We reposition to see ourselves*
> *from another angle, but then,*
> *we are no longer there to be seen.*

> In the final experiment, you float on an
> air balloon, overseeing the ocean, the
> mountain, the glacier, the river, the empty
> square, the skyscraper, the carnival. I
> point my weapon of choice at you. I don't
> fire.

We let our identities explode into names, plans, promises. We know rock, steel, paint, eye, arm, back. Other stories invade our lives. The war starts, the war ends. Mysteries are solved and unsolved. The protagonist sleeps through the rest of it, uncertain in which story to build a life. The dog runs in with a toy in its mouth.

In the final experiment, the protagonist
is the protagonist. The protagonist
hesitates to enter, walks away, aware that
the narrative deals with matters of life
and death. It's not worth a quarter. The
protagonist's tall figure recedes.

We've felt unnoticed so long we
burn to leap into familiarity.

We are wrapped inside a bundle of narratives. Bright sun, bright moon.
And our own story – so beautiful, so ready to end. Veins have no traffic
rules, no rest stops. Outside the frame, the protagonist sighs with relief. We
try to stay asleep, but at dawn we wake to see the sun, real or fake. We dive
into day with each other's faces in mind.

In the final experiment, you are the
protagonist, and I'm the author. You
resent the implications of this assignment.
You discard every copy of my account.
You pick up a pen and write.

◇ 3 ◇

THE MELTING HOURGLASS

◇ 3 ◇

THE MELTING HOURGLASS

I am an hourglass
most of me before
some after
almost none
in the narrow
now

Goombeldt walks in
folding his umbrella
why is he carrying an umbrella?
it's not raining

Zungvilda is not home yet

glaciers melt in trickles
and flood the earth

can the umbrella protect
from the flood?

Zungvilda might be in orbit
perpetually spinning the earth
like the moon's beautiful competitor
or she might be riding an imaginary bike
following imaginary rules
along a river not yet imagined

Goombeldt sits by the window
counting the raindrops in his memory
raindrops that hit the ground
in rains long past

I am here too
but I remain unnoticed
invisibility suits me
since I gained all this weight
the weight of centuries
stretched ahead
so crudely
devoid
of me

each new memory
brings new forgetting
futures unravel
at the speed of chance

you are nearby
like you always are

we share our distance

I cannot see you
I cannot hear you
I never will

Zungvilda shares her thoughts
I have no choice but to listen
after all she lives inside my head

she asks why men are so difficult
don't generalize I say
but she can't hear me in there

I'm afraid it's a monologue
I'm afraid it always is

she wonders why every day seems to start
with wild yanking and smoke
like an old lawn mower
she muses about the interchangeable
questions and answers

she suspects that the new crater
that just formed on the moon
might be her early grave
she remembers the time

when she was a girl
lost in the forest

I remember it too
even though I was
too young to remember

Dear Reader
I remember the
shore the
palms the
waves the smell the
smile the
grimace the
dead man's
face

and now
you remember it too

Dear Reader
you remember
the ice
the moon
the shovel
the frozen bodies

and now
I've been there

here in the trench
under crude bombardment
the only thing Goombeldt can think of
is a dying plant on his windowsill
a souvenir of Zungvilda's past presence

they could barely speak
barely look at each other
the plant the only thing alive
between them

it is dead by now
most certainly dried out
by the moon's gravity
tugging
at the sea of forgetting

the plant is just a twig of dust
under crude bombardment
for the rest of our lives

Zungvilda is at the seashore
of her childhood
Goombeldt climbs the mountain
of his choice
the moon stares indifferently
invisible behind its camouflage
of the midday sun

I put a comma
in the wrong place
I moved the scalpel
the wrong way

the world will
never be
the same

you watch me
through the lens of a telescope
my shining eyes magnified

you know me
you trust me
you run to me

there's no one here

you stop
puzzled

inverted

hours turn to glass
as I watch you
through the lens of a telescope

you open your umbrella on a sunny day
and who am I to judge you
it never rains around here

there was a flood

you hid in the bathtub
you opened the drain
you waited
for all the world's water
to go down
so you could breathe

your bathtub became
an umbrella

you flew away

I remember you
I imagine you
as Goombeldt and Zungvilda
imagine each other

we die

were we ever real
if we couldn't stay real?

the world recycles its time
sand's tongue licks the narrow tube
of the hourglass

the sea of forgetting listens
as we play out,
notes in a long song

Zungvilda is on the train
between two selves
Goombeldt
somewhere else in the universe

how curved lives can be

last time she saw him
his smile was endless
frozen on his face

if other planets exist
there is one
where we start from scratch

outside on the platform
you said something distant
something that puzzled me

Zungvilda tries to open
the window
rain licks the glass
like thoughts from long ago

we expose the negatives
in one another
in the light we share

we live exposed

I lived with you
then I died
you have no choice
but to remember me

Zungvilda is on a battlefield
under crude bombardment
she folds her umbrella
and puts it away

if only the rest of the world
were this collapsible

I retreat into my past
swallow my memories

just recently
we still could change

Zungvilda is taking a bath
floating in a pool of raindrops
Goombeldt is on a battlefield
under crude bombardment

Dear Reader
I unwrap myself
like a delicate candy
but to whose tongue
does it belong?
is there anything left
after the wrapper?

Goombeldt
makes fun of me
as if he
were any more concrete

Dear Reader
you are in a well-lit room
you remember the snow
the ice
the smile the grimace
on the dead man's face

Dear Reader
I am a raindrop
falling upward
a thought years ago
somewhere
that doesn't exist

Zungvilda is half-present
hiding behind memories
behind raindrops
from rains long past

I asked
Goombeldt and Zungvilda
if they were the same person

they just smiled in response

what about you?
are you the same person?

if I'm the negative
then who's the image?

you said something distant
something I missed

as usual
from my perspective
you are far ahead
of me

I think of you
and I turn into an icicle
I'm like glass
but made of water

Zungvilda's wrinkles in the mirror
like sand dunes

time is not smooth

if you don't mind
I'll grow into an iceberg
and reflect more light

Goombeldt's hair
turns gray

one grain of sand at a time

we belong together
in our half-world
you've been an iceberg
all along

the hourglass of my life
    is melting

an elusive shape

how strange
each day
a melted replica of another

how strange
the glass itself
was made
of
sand
and breath

I put a comma in the wrong place
must I pay the price?

I ran out of breath
before I ran
out of time

how strange
Zungvilda and Goombeldt
don't seem to care

Dear Reader
mysteries occur
before we notice
and futures unravel
at the speed of choice
each move
unfolds centuries
with each step
the sea of forgetting
follows

Dear Reader
outside on the platform
you said something meaningful

something I missed

under crude bombardment
I ask Zungvilda some questions

whose fault was it?
what went wrong?

but when the smoke clears
I see it's Goombeldt
I've been talking to

and what's the difference
my own female self
is with me now
and every minute

may we cancel
the bombardment?

may we open the moon?
fold our umbrellas
and enter?

flip the hourglass
it's no one's fault
nothing went wrong

when I saw you last
you were so small
like a raindrop
with an IV

yet over the years
you have grown
in my memory

when it's my turn
to be a raindrop
will you welcome me
into your ocean?

° 4 °

YOUR LIFE AS IT IS

You wake up in the morning.
You go outside.
This is your life as it is.

You wake up in the morning and get out of bed. The carnival is in town. The signs are unmistakable. The calliope song. The smells. The excited voices.

Your husband is making breakfast. He is humming to himself. You would rather have silence, but you will not say anything.

> *Last year's footprint is this year's mudslide. The pawns are running an election to select the king. You receive your own radio transmission from the future. It is encrypted, you don't know the cipher yet.*

You go outside. The bright red sunset is the same as the last time.

You wake up in the morning. A blind woman is standing over your bed, her face impassive, her hands folded on her chest. She is wearing a blue dress, the kind of blue only a repressed human being could invent.

Instead of saying anything, you just keep staring. You know she knows you are no longer asleep. Your wife is using her sewing machine: the tender percussion of racing stitches.

> *Your former future has become your recent past. Promises should be taken as good intentions: that's the only way to play it safe. The king is no longer interested in being the center of attention. You emit signals only those who don't care about you will notice.*

You go outside. You want to ask the blind woman what she is doing here, but when you open your mouth, she is gone. You must be asleep, but she is convinced that you are not.

You wake up in the morning. Nothing is out of the ordinary. You count to one hundred. This is the time you allow yourself before you get out of bed and start your day.

Your dog runs in with a toy in his mouth. He wants to play. But you have too much to do. You pet him absentmindedly. The hair on his muzzle is gray, just like you remember it.

> *Your interaction with yourself assumes the form of monologue. You often refer to yourself as he. You refer to others too infrequently. The king walks off the board, indifferent to the battle other pieces wage. The radio transmission disclosed that something was missing, and now you know what it is. You are a blind person.*

You go outside. It is raining. It has been raining for days. The rain is the sound it makes, your wet hair. You try to imagine what it might look like, but you have no frame of reference.

You wake up in the morning. There will come an age when the fact of a new awakening is a gift in and of itself. But you are blissfully far from that point. You wonder if the carnival is in town—you listen for the familiar sounds, but they are missing. It must not be the time yet. Then you remember about your hearing loss.

Your brother has not written for a month or two. You are going through your recent interactions to determine if you may have inadvertently offended him. People always arrive at wrong conclusions.

> *Your past is like a streetlight at midnight. Your wishes evolve into acceptance. The queen is unhappy that the king is getting all the attention, but she wouldn't want to be in his shoes. Your successes may be indicative of your failure to relax.*

You go outside. The blind woman is nowhere to be seen. You are relieved that you don't have to encounter her today. She may be asleep.

You wake up in the morning. Getting out of bed is the last thing you want to do. It is snowing, the trees are beautiful and indifferent, their white foliage immaterial like your life.

You hear a child's voice, half-singing half-mumbling. For a moment, you can't remember if it's your own child, whether it's a boy or a girl. You may still be asleep. You wonder if you should get up and dive into your life. Perhaps you have more time to linger.

> *Your past is your present turned inside out. There is nothing awaiting you that you have not already imagined. A factual achievement may not be superior to an imaginary one. The bishop is tired of diagonals. He longs for the white fields, so close and so inaccessible. An intense, passionate existence may not be a good recipe for a superior afterlife.*

You go outside. The snow is gone, the trees have turned green. Perhaps you were looking out the wrong window. The child's voice you heard just a minute ago disappears. The child must have grown up. Next, your house disappears. You too may have reached adulthood. You keep walking.

You wake up in the morning and find yourself in the middle of a snow-covered field. Minuscule on the horizon stands an outline of the place you call home. The only path you can see leads away from it.

Your husband is walking toward you across the vast distance. His figure is tiny, but his enormous shining eyes are like moons over the spare landscape.

Somewhere along the way your smile turned into a grimace. You have tried to mark your every turn so you can make your way out of the labyrinth. But the paint has run out. Knights and bishops are laughing at you from a nearby hill. Then you notice that the walls are two feet high. If you hadn't looked down all your life you would have realized this sooner.

You go outside. The street is brightly decorated. Cheerful balloons of all colors are tied to benches, street signs, even the parked cars. But there is no one in sight. It is possible that the whole world exists exclusively for your sake.

You wake up in the morning. The carnival sounds you heard just a minute ago belong to your dream. The waking life is the same as the dream, but without the carnival. You have to warm up your car.

Your wife was supposed to make the tea, but the thermos is empty. You get upset, but when you check on her, her body is rounded onto itself. You touch her forehead. It's cold and impenetrable like other dreams that have slipped away. You don't have to close her eyes.

Your handwriting had turned illegible before arriving on paper. This is the nature of your thoughts. A black and white couple of pawns get married and improvise a new game.

You go outside. The little girl rides her bicycle by your front porch. The wheels are frozen, as if she is in a film. You realize you too may be in a film. You look around for a camera, but your own eyes are the camera and the source of light.

You wake up in the morning and find yourself floating in the middle of an ocean. You should be worried, but strangely enough, you are not. You know there must exist a current that will take you home.

Your daughter did not do her homework, and now everything may be lost. She was sent home without lunch and without the right to a bright future. You suspect that your own punishment will be even more severe.

The mysteries you puzzled over have not been solved, but they have become irrelevant. The queen underwent transgender surgery, rendering your pieces defenseless against your opponent. You have forgotten who your opponent is.

You go outside. The sun is bright. The blind woman is at the street corner. She looks as if she is waiting for you. Her expression makes you uneasy—you know she is aware of your presence. "Where are you going?" she asks. You wish you knew.

You wake up in the morning. The world's silence puzzles you. The birds, the cars and the ocean all decided to take a break at the same time. Then you remember about your recent hearing loss. The sounds you heard in your dreams were transmissions from the past.

Your wife is drifting on a block of ice, carried by the fast current of a black river. She is waving to you in horror, only a few solid inches around her separating her from a cold, liquid death. You are running along the riverbank, trying to keep up. You know you must do something to save her, but you are not sure what. You stop to tie your shoes.

> *Your plans have become memories of plans. You missed the moment when this transition took place. Recently you had a way out of this predicament. You shared your escape strategy with a rook, and now every pawn knows all about it, even though you have forgotten.*

You go outside. The simple truths of air, trees, sky, ground are no longer satisfactory, nor undeniable. You find yourself floating over the earth, your body horizontal. You can see both the sky and the land without turning around.

You wake up in the morning. The blind man is sitting on the edge of your bed, swaying in rhythm to the sounds of a song only he can hear. It's odd to see tears streaming down from his eyes. You did not expect faulty eyes to retain some of their functionality.

Your wife walks in and speaks to you, but you don't register her words. You must still be half asleep. You are surprised that she pays the blind man absolutely no attention, as if his presence here were not unexpected.

> *Your yesterday's song has become today's avalanche. The roaring waves of snow eliminate all obstacles in your path. You think about it for a moment and realize that it is, in fact, someone else's path. The pawns glare at you in condemnation before being swept away.*

You go outside. The tranquility of this summer morning reminds you that life is essentially peaceful. All you have to do is lean into it, let it carry you along. But you have become too heavy from the sadness and the pessimism that stick to you as you advance through time.

You wake up in the morning. You are happy to see another day unfolding before you. There is much to do and see. You had plans for today, but at the moment, all of them seem utterly unimportant. You decide to improvise.

Your son is humming a tune in the next room, something vague under his breath. The melody is familiar, but hard as you try, you can't place it. When you enter the room, it's empty. You remember what happened to your son.

> The king is mad about having to spend the entire game undercover. You did not play it safe. You made a mistake of wanting too much from the world. Your friends are happy with their enjoyable, less demanding lives. You don't have any friends.

You go outside. The carnival crew is packing. An ending packs more emotional energy than a beginning. All endings are preconceived. The birds sound as if they disagree with this simple fact.

You wake up in the morning without a frame of reference. People always arrive at wrong conclusions. Since your dog died, you find your monologues empty, as if every statement you make has already been uttered by someone else, in a more appropriate context.

You remember the last time you traveled abroad. The buzzing crowds whose language you could not understand intimidated you. You have remained in your own town ever since, unwilling to give up your familiar comforts.

> When you listen carefully, the words you will say during your remaining days can be heard as soft, hesitant whispers. If you could hear them, you would learn how to avoid the pitfalls that are otherwise inescapable. You know you will have to wait for that knowledge to arrive too late. The king and the queen are in bed, laughing at you.

You go outside. The house you have always lived in has been replaced by another building. You wonder whether you will be able to reenter your life by going inside anyway, but you are too afraid to try it. The bells of a missing church resound nearby.

You wake up in the morning. A boom microphone is placed over your bed, and in the window, a poorly concealed camera muzzle can be seen.

Perhaps there is a better way—one you have not thought of. The best answers to your questions always come to others. Your silence is not your own. Your family, real and imaginary, owns all the answers.

Your blind eyes hunger for visual information. A hope that one day you might miraculously regain your sight has never quite left you, despite the utter absurdity of such a hope. You have heard that inexplicable things are likely to happen at a moment's notice. The knights suffer from neck pain caused by the crooked moves they are forced to make.

You go outside and find yourself on a rapidly moving train. A little boy peeks at you from the seat ahead. When you smile to him, he flashes a return smile and hides his face. Life is a series of curious glances, exploratory words, shy smiles.

You wake up in the morning. A strange sound penetrates your room. You have to focus to understand what it is. A child, crying. You must have done something to cause the child's unhappiness. You try to remember if you have a child of your own. You wonder why it is so easy to assume guilt.

Your husband is using his power tools in the shed, and you realize you are completely uninterested in his current endeavor. This is what it means to love someone for a long time.

> Your memory is like a fake fairy tale, reenacted. The queen smiles and takes off her clothes. Then she takes off her skin, and finally her flesh. Her skeleton is both a question mark and an exclamation point.

You go outside. The snow has melted before falling again. The world looks as if nothing had changed. This is what happens when changes replace changes. You close your eyes.

You wake up in the morning. The mysteries of your life are encoded with a cipher that is vaguely familiar, yet the precise clue eludes you. It would help if you could understand more about it, but as things stand, you seem to understand less and less.

The child that was crying earlier has quieted. Unexpectedly, the silence is unsettling. You worry that something tragic may have happened. Something tragic always happens, but most of the time these events take place elsewhere.

> *The sounds you can no longer hear cut through your deafness. The images of things you can no longer see have taken up permanent residence in your mind. You have heard and seen enough. The king and the queen are dancing a slow dance in your memory. You often refer to yourself as she and forget about others.*

You go outside. The snow has been falling all night, and now the path to the gate is completely covered. There may be no gate, and most likely, there is no house. You are naked. You must invent another way to survive.

You wake up in the morning. The world feels strange in some intangible way. You lie with your eyes closed, trying to determine what is causing this impression. The universe may be different, but on the other hand, the difference may be wholly within you.

Your mother used to look at you disapprovingly. Since her death, you have no way to determine whether her criticism was your problem or her own. You wish you could ask her several simple questions that are always on the tip of your tongue.

> A pawn is conspiring to make it all the way across the board, causing a conflict of interest in the queen's mind. The king has fallen asleep. The radio transmission you are trying to send is not properly encoded. You must seek help if you want it to make sense upon reception.

You go outside. You feel you may be forgetting something important. The vast green field is swaying in the wind, unaware of the fact that it is a black and white photograph taken in winter.

You wake up in the morning. The little boy is standing by your bed with a question on his lips, but he is mute, and you can't lip-read. You need an interpreter, but the world eludes interpretation.

Your sister is lost in a vast field covered with snow. You try to rescue her, but your feet become the tip of a pencil and the field, a sheet of paper. You realize you must write something significant, but to do so, you must learn a language. Your handwriting alone might not suffice without words.

> *Your opponent has been making much progress, but it's not an issue: you have resigned yourself to a life without a bright future. You suspect you may be a pawn, but there is something heavy mounted on your head. Your smiles have become deflated from exposure. Tomorrow you will need to be yourself, perhaps for the first time.*

You go outside. The blind man aims a gun at you, and you know that your chances of escape are immaterial like a kiss from an affair you had when you were young. Now the world itself is young, but you have grown old.

You wake up in the morning and open your eyes. Your room is crowded. Your old friends, long dead, have come to honor you. Their eyes are kind, as if they had forgiven you all the offenses you unwittingly committed.

Your husband desperately holds on to a tree branch suspended over a deep canyon. You stand on the edge. You want to help, but as much as you try, you can't reach him. In panic, you scan the area for something you could use to help him hold his weight. There is nothing but pinecones and dry leaves. You bend over to tie your shoes.

> *The king and the queen have retired. They took up residence off the board. You can see their house from your front porch. The smoke from their barbeque causes you to tear up in fake grief.*

You go outside. The heavy orange sky is oppressive like a dying love affair. The day must be ending. You missed its beginning. You missed many things you would have loved.

You wake up in the morning. The clouds outside your window are strangely immobile, as if they were painted on the glass. Perhaps the wind is still asleep. You realize it would be nice to do something meaningful today, but no specific ideas come to mind.

Your husband's car is still in the driveway. You are surprised he has not left for work. It's not like him. You walk out into the living room and find him resting on your beautiful hardwood floor. You don't feel anything at the thought of his absence.

> *Your skin is a reflection of your attempts to get closer to the true meaning of your life, but you suspect that it might be inside out. The bishop has given up faith and no longer finds satisfaction in diagonal existence. You remember your own memories better than your past.*

You walk outside and find yourself on another street, next to another house. You might have been a different person all along, or perhaps there is a better explanation for all of this.

You wake up in the morning, but it's dark outside. You could be in the far North. The stars are all missing. The world must have run out of light. Everything is encrypted, and you don't know the cipher yet.

You were willing to share your time with others, but others did not share with you. Your supplies have run dry. The blind person is at the end of the block, waving a cane. You know the signals are meant for you. You can't remember how you concluded this.

> *The smile on the king's face is guarded, as if he were trying to encourage you without offering any concrete guarantees. The ambulance arrives to pick up the pawns wounded in the battle. You receive a transmission from the past, but you can't remember who sent it.*

You go outside. Then you realize that you have forgotten all your things. You want to go back in, but the door through which you came out is missing, replaced by a concrete wall. You are completely naked on a windy street.

You wake up in the morning. You are in the middle of a vast empty square, sharp nails of skyscrapers piercing the clouds. You must be here for a meeting, but you can't remember with whom. The buildings are identical.

Your dead mother is surprised to see you. Her lips move, but no sound is produced. You realize that you have gone deaf. You try to read her lips, but they don't appear to form words. You take her by the hand to guide her out of this place. Her hand is small.

> *Your history is more ancient with every day. Before a moment passes, it is already registered in the catalog of the past. The catalog is not alphabetized. A few pawns are picking on a rook in the space between the ocean and the river.*

You go outside, but the outside is gone. It's like a vast empty field, but without a field. It's like you, but without you. You have brought a library of building blocks from which you will construct it all over, every day. You must create yourself and the world around you. This is your life as it is.

ACKNOWLEDGMENTS:

Selections from "The Melting Hourglass" published by *Allbook Books*, *Rusty Truck* and *Folded Word*.

"The Catalog of Broken Things" published by *The Raleigh Review*

"Your Life as It Is" published by *Accents Publishing*, Editor's Choice winner in their 2014 poetry chapbook contest.

■

"Your Life as It Is" was written on a trip to Russia in May 2011.

Special thanks to Laura Stahman for her conceptual and editorial suggestions, and for her support throughout the writing of this book.

Thank you to Annie Lighthart for introducing me to Airlie Press.

I'm especially grateful to Beth Ford for her patience and inspiration with the cover image.

I'm most indebted to fellow Airlie poets for their comments: Deborah Akers, Jon Boisvert, Karen McPherson, Darlene Pagán, Tim Shaner, Kelly Terwilliger, Tim Whitsel.

Thanks to John Sibley Williams for his detailed review and suggestions for "The Melting Hourglass."

With deep gratitude to the members of The Guttery and The Moonlit Poetry Caravan for their help with some of the poems: Dale Baker, April Curfman, Brenna Dimmig, Jamie Duclos-Yourdon, Bruce Greene, Juleen Johnson, Josh Keen, Jennifer Lesh, Janis Lull, Tracy Manaster, Beth Marshea, Emily Newberry, Brian Reeves, Cameron M. Smith, Mark Struzan, Carrie-Ann Tkaczyk, Robin Troche, Jeff Whitney.

ABOUT THE PUBLISHER

Airlie Press is run by writers. A nonprofit publishing collective, the press is dedicated to producing beautiful and compelling books of poetry. Its mission is to offer a shared-work publishing alternative for writers working in the Pacific Northwest. Airlie Press is supported by book sales and donations. All funds return to the press for the creation of new books of poetry.

COLOPHON

Titles are set in Cormorant SC. Poems are set in Cormorant Light. Cormorant is a contemporary display serif typeface inspired by the Garamond heritage, hand-drawn and produced by Catharsis Fonts. Printed in Portland, Oregon on 30% post-consumer recycled paper.